AF292041

The RYA is the UK governing body representing sailing, windsurfing, motor boating, and personal watercraft, at sea and on inland waters. It works for the good of all who enjoy these activities, campaigning for their interests at local, regional, national, European, and world level.

For information on the RYA's

- Training courses
- Coaching schemes
- Free technical, legal, and general advice
- Books and other products

or to support our work and gain valuable benefits by becoming a personal member, please visit our website at **www.rya.org.uk**.

You can re-order RYA Wet Notes from the RYA webshop www.rya.org.uk/shop or by calling the order hotline on 02380 604 132.
Printed in the UK